# The Darkness Within

Melanie Fleming

BookLeaf Publishing

India | USA | UK

The Darkness Within © 2022 Melanie Fleming

All rights reserved.



Melanie Fleming asserts the moral right to be identified as author of this work.

Presentation by *BookLeaf Publishing*

Web: www.bookleafpub.com

E-mail: info@bookleafpub.com

ISBN: 9789357214360

First edition 2022

# Wings

The desire to soar above the mundane ignites my
soul,
Yet my wings are clipped,
Static, I remain.

# Our Story

Our future is unwritten,
Who's holding the pen?
I wonder if we're in the same book, let alone on
the same chapter or page.

But then I remember that I never unfolded the
corner that holds 'Our Story',
For it was one of my favourites,
And I couldn't have chosen a better co-author.

# Breathe

There's a tightness in my chest.
Relinquished control of my lungs.
Environmental tranquillity provides no comfort.
Animosity is felt towards strangers that can
handle the minutiae of life.
Inhale...hold...exhale.

# The Search

Who am I in this world?
Where do I belong?
What's my purpose?
Am I worth it?
Will I never follow my hearts song?

It's still beating in my chest,
It's my mind that will not rest,
Seeking answers to questions that make life feel
like a test.

# Social Reject

I can see behind your diamond eyes, you're
haunted by clouded skies above.
Broken and collecting dust, like a rag doll on the
shelf.

Your sense of self trapped in the past,
Illusions of happiness didn't last,
Feeling inadequate.

They try to help you - You're not listening!
They knock on your door - But you won't let
them in!

Please believe me when I tell you the future's
unwritten, and there is hope yet for the social
reject.

# Monsters

The worst monsters are in my head,
Not underneath my bed,
Not lurking in the shadows,
But in my brain instead.

# The Escape Artist

Discovering their portrayal was a lie,
A camouflaged enemy locking me in a prison of
my own emotions.
In solitary confinement my sanity slipped
through my fingers.
As I forced a smile to the world, I had no clear
solution.
I was just an unsuccessful escape artist.

# Just Friends

They say it's better to be friends than nothing at
all,
But what if that persons love is what you're
longing for?
As feelings are buried and emotions are raw,
Anxiously wondering if we'll ever be more,
than 'just friends'.

# Unobtainable Love

As tough as nature can command my spirit to be,
I am not a master of deception,
Thus cannot camouflage my emotions.

My heart yearns for permanency,
Yet only the sea is certain to collide with
intention against the rocks.

I have fallen in unobtainable love.

# Stone Heart

My heart of gold is turning to stone once again,
So I can protect my soul from eternal torment.

Preservation of sanity against societal
expectations of my gift wrapped happiness that
ceases to exist.

# Sunflowers and Daisy Chains

Am I truly your Sunflower?
Or just another Daisy in the chain?

For if I am your Sunflower, I thrive in the
warmth of your light,
Turning toward you to help me bloom.

Yet a daisy lacks significance,
Picked for momentary appreciation before its
disposal,

# Wrong Direction

Out of sight is out of mind,
But there's no pause or rewind.
Been through this a thousand times,
I can't leave the past behind.
Poisoned with your lies,
An enemy disguised,
Trying to creep your way back home,
But you're heading the wrong way.

# Carnival Games

Welcome to the Carnival of Love!
Do you see the red flags?
Follow them into the distance and let the games
begin.

Let's go catch myself a victim,
Hook a duck and claim my prize,
I'm the ring master,
A wolf in sheep's clothing hiding in plain sight.

You belong in the circus,
I've treated you like a clown,
Throwing love bombs at the dunk tank in which
you'll surely drown.

# Serpent's Mirage

Trust is nothing but a for the traveller wandering the desert in search of salvation.

The sands of love intertwined with deception concealed a serpent carrying venom to poison my judgement with a slim mouth adorning a silver tongue.

# Devil's Tango

Come along and dance with me,
In the shade of the broken,
Bleeding tears upon the flames of our existence.

Slow stepping the corridors of troubled minds,
Familiar winds of nonreciprocal intent
extinguish the passion within.

Isolation arose from unity in the form of an
addiction,
One more romance before collapsing to our
knees at the hand of the unworthy owners of the
purest souls.

# Crazy Diamond

My Crazy Diamond,
You fail to see how you glimmer in the sunlight.
The rarity of the beauty you possess.
And though times are hard,
Your spirit cannot be broken,
For diamonds are formed under stress.

# Nihilist Dreams

Society has become selfish,
Our youth have a death wish,
Media sets unrealistic goals without the means
to accomplish.

So I wear my heart on my sleeve,
In true love I want to believe,
Yet a thousand reasons make my soul scream!

Why does everyone I get close to leave?
Does the problem reside in me?
Or are happy endings just nihilist dreams?

I'm no closer to the answers,
Anxiety is that bastard,
Keeping me in a state of searching without a
light on.

# Unarmed Warrior

Spoon fed love licked off a knifes edge that
would later etch crimson rivers upon my skin.
Each line a permanent reminded of surrendering
the blade.
An unarmed warrior is born.